THE ILLUSTRATED POETS

Robert Burns

EDITED BY
Daniel Burnstone

This is a Parragon Book.
Produced by Magpie Books,
an imprint of Robinson Publishing, London

Parragon
Unit 13-17, Avonbridge Trading Estate,
Atlantic Road, Avonmouth,
Bristol, BS11 9QD

Reprinted 1996

Cover picture: *Robert Burns* by Alexander Naysmith; Scottish National Portrait Gallery, Edinburgh/Bridgeman Art Gallery. Illustrations courtesy of: Scottish Writers Museum; Mary Evans Picture Library; Christies Images.

ISBN 0 75250 026 0

A copy of the British Library Cataloguing in Publication Data is available from the British Library.

Typeset by Hewer Text Composition Services, Edinburgh
Printed in Singapore by Tien Wah Press

Contents

❧ DRINK AND THE DEVIL ☙

To William Stewart

In honest Bacon's ingle-neuk,
  Here maun I sit and think;
Sick o' the warld and warld's fock,
  And sick, d-mn'd sick o' drink!

I see, I see there is nae help,
  But still down I maun sink;
Till some day, *laigh enough*, I yelp,
  'Wae worth that cursed drink!'

Yestreen, alas! I was sae fu',
  I could but yisk and wink;
And now, this day, sair, sair I rue,
  The weary, weary drink. –

Satan, I fear thy sooty claws,
  I hate thy brunstane stink,
And ay I curse the luckless cause,
  The wicked soup o' drink. –

In vain I would forget my woes
  In idle rhyming clink,
For past redemption d-mn'd in Prose
  I can do nought but drink. –

For you, my trusty, well-try'd friend,
  May Heaven still on you blink;
And may your life flow to the end,
  Sweet as a dry man's drink!

Scotch Drink

Gie him strong drink, until he wink,
That's sinking in despair;
An' liquor guid to fire his bluid,
That's prest wi' grief an' care;
There let him bouse, an' deep carouse,
Wi' bumpers flowing o'er,
Till he forgets his loves or debts,
An' minds his griefs no more.
SOLOMON (Proverbs xxxi, 6, 7)

Let other Poets raise a fracas
'Bout vines, an' wines, an' drunken Bacchus,
An' crabbèd names an' stories wrack us,
An' grate our lug;
I sing the juice Scotch bear can mak us,
In glass or jug.

O thou, my Muse! guid auld Scotch Drink,
Whether thro' wimplin worms thou jink,
Or, richly brown, ream owre the brink,
In glorious faem;
Inspire me, till I lisp an' wink,
To sing thy name!

Let husky wheat the haughs adorn,
An's aits set up their awnie horn,
An' pease an' beans at een or morn,
Perfume the plain;
Leeze me on thee, John Barleycorn,
Thou King o' grain!

On thee aft Scotland chows her cood,
In souple scones, the wale o' food!
Or tumblin' in the boiling flood
Wi' kail an' beef;
But when thou pours thy strong heart's blood,
There thou shines chief.

Food fills the wame, an' keeps us livin';
Tho' life's a gift no worth receivin',
When heavy-dragg'd wi' pine an' grievin';
But, oil'd by thee,
The wheels o' life gae down-hill, scrievin'
Wi' rattlin' glee.

Thou clears the head o' doited Lear:
Thou cheers the heart o' drooping Care;
Thou strings the nerves o' Labour sair,
At's weary toil:
Thou even brightens dark Despair
Wi' gloomy smile.

Aft, clad in massy siller weed,
Wi' gentles thou erects thy head;
Yet humbly kind, in time o' need,
The poor man's wine,
His wee drap parritch, or his bread,
Thou kitchens fine.

Thou art the life o' public haunts;
But thee, what were our fairs and rants?
Ev'n godly meetings o' the saunts,
By thee inspir'd,
When gaping they besiege the tents,
Are doubly fir'd.

That merry night we get the corn in!
O sweetly then thou reams the horn in!
Or reekin' on a New-Year mornin'
In cog or bicker,
An' just a wee drap sp'ritual burn in,
An' gusty sucker!

When Vulcan gies his bellows breath,
An' ploughmen gather wi' their graith,
O rare to see thee fizz an' freath
I' th' luggèd caup!
Then Burnewin comes on like death
At ev'ry chaup.

Nae mercy, then, for airn or steel;
The brawnie, banie, ploughman chiel,
Brings hard owrehip, wi' sturdy wheel,
The strong forehammer,
Till block an' studdio ring an' reel
Wi' dinsome clamour.

When skirlin' weanies see the light,
Thou maks the gossips-clatter bright
How fumblin' cuifs their dearies slight –
Wae worth the name!
Nae Howdie gets a social night,
Or plack frae them.

When neibors anger at a plea,
An' just as wud as wud can be,
How easy can the barley-bree
Cement the quarrel!
It's aye the cheapest lawyer's fee
To taste the barrel.

Alake! that e'er my Muse has reason
To wyte her countrymen wi' treason;
But mony daily weet their weasan'
Wi' liquors nice,
An' hardly, in a winter's season,
E'er spier her price.

Wae worth that brandy, burning trash!
Fell source o' mony a pain an' brash!
Twins mony a poor, doylt, drucken hash,
O' half his days;
An' sends, beside, auld Scotland's cash
To her warst faes.

Ye Scots, wha wish auld Scotland well,
Ye chief, to you my tale I tell,
Poor plackless devils like mysel'!
            It sets you ill,
Wi' bitter, dearthfu' wines to mell,
            Or foreign gill,

May gravels round his blather wrench,
An' gouts torment him, inch by inch,
Wha twists his gruntle wi' a glunch
            O' sour disdain,
Out owre a glass o' whisky punch
            Wi' honest men!

O Whisky! soul o' plays an' pranks!
Accept a bardie's gratefu' thanks!
When wanting thee, what tuneless cranks
Are my poor verses!
Thou comes – they rattle i' their ranks
At ither's arses!

Thee, Ferintosh! O sadly lost!
Scotland, lament frae coast to coast!
Now colic-grips an' barkin' hoast
May kill us a';
For loyal Forbes' charter'd boast
Is ta'en awa!

Thae curst horse-leeches o' th' Excise,
Wha mak the whisky stells their prize –
Haud up thy hand, deil! Ance – twice – thrice!
There, seize the blinkers!
An' bake them up in brunstane pies
For poor damn'd drinkers.

Fortune! if thou'll but gie me still
Hale breeks, a bannock, and a gill,
An' rowth o' rhyme to rave at will,
Tak' a' the rest,
An' deal'd about as thy blind skill
Directs thee best.

Burns' birthplace near Ayr

Tam O' Shanter

When chapman billies leave the street,
And drouthy neibors neibors meet,
As market-days are wearing late,
An' folk begin to tak the gate;
While we sit bousing at the nappy,
An' getting fou and unco happy,
We think na on the lang Scots miles,
The mosses, waters, slaps, and styles,
That lie between us and our hame,
Where sits our sulky sullen dame,
Gathering her brows like gathering storm,
Nursing her wrath to keep it warm.
  This truth fand honest Tam o' Shanter,
As he frae Ayr ae night did canter –
(Auld Ayr, wham ne'er a town surpasses
For honest men and bonnie lasses).

O Tam! hadst thou but been sae wise
As ta'en thy ain wife Kate's advice!
She tauld thee weel thou was a skellum,
A bletherin', blusterin', drunken blellum;
That frae November till October,
Ae market-day thou was na sober;
That ilka melder wi' the miller
Thou sat as lang as thou had siller;
That every naig was ca'd a shoe on,
The smith and thee gat roarin' fou on;
That at the Lord's house, even on Sunday,
Thou drank wi' Kirkton Jean till Monday.
She prophesied that, late or soon,
Thou would be found deep drown'd in Doon;
Or catch'd wi' warlocks in the mirk
By Alloway's auld haunted kirk.

Ah, gentle dames! it gars me greet
To think how mony counsels sweet,
How mony lengthen'd sage advices,
The husband frae the wife despises!

But to our tale: Ae market night,
Tam had got planted unco right,
Fast by an ingle, bleezing finely,
Wi' reaming swats, that drank divinely;
And at his elbow, Souter Johnny,
His ancient, trusty, drouthy crony;
Tam lo'ed him like a very brither;
They had been fou for weeks thegither.
The night drave on wi' sangs and clatter,
And aye the ale was growing better:
The landlady and Tam grew gracious,
Wi' favours secret, sweet, and precious;
The souter tauld his queerest stories;
The landlord's laugh was ready chorus:
The storm without might rair and rustle,
Tam did na mind the storm a whistle.

Care, mad to see a man sae happy,
E'en drown'd himsel amang the nappy.
As bees flee hame wi' lades o' treasure,
The minutes wing'd their way wi' pleasure;
Kings may be blest, but Tam was glorious,
O'er a' the ills o' life victorious!

But pleasures are like poppies spread –
You seize the flow'r, its bloom is shed;
Or like the snow falls in the river –
A moment white, then melts for ever;
Or like the borealis race,
That flit ere you can point their place;
Or like the rainbow's lovely form
Evanishing amid the storm.
Nae man can tether time nor tide;
The hour approaches Tam maun ride;
That hour, o' night's black arch the key-stane,
That dreary hour, he mounts his beast in;
And sic a night he taks the road in,
As ne'er poor sinner was abroad in.

Tam O'Shanter at Alloway Kirk, William Carse

The wind blew as 'twad blawn its last;
The rattling show'rs rose on the blast;
The speedy gleams the darkness swallow'd;
Loud, deep, and lang, the thunder bellow'd:
That night, a child might understand,
The Deil had business on his hand.

Weel mounted on his gray mare, Meg,
A better never lifted leg,
Tam skelpit on thro' dub and mire,
Despising wind, and rain, and fire;
Whiles holding fast his gude blue bonnet;
Whiles crooning o'er some auld Scots sonnet;
Whiles glow'ring round wi' prudent cares,
Lest bogles catch him unawares.
Kirk-Alloway was drawing nigh,
Whare ghaists adn houlets nightly cry.

By this time he was cross the ford,
Where in the snaw the chapman smoor'd;
And past the birks and meikle stane,
Where drunken Charlie brak's neck-bane;

And thro' the whins, and by the cairn,
Where hunters fand the murder'd bairn;
And near the thorn, aboon the well,
Where Mungo's mither hang'd hersel.
Before him Doon pours all his floods;
The doubling storm roars thro' the woods;
The lightnings flash from pole to pole;
Near and more near the thunders roll:
When, glimmering thro' the groaning trees,
Kirk-Alloway seem'd in a bleeze;
Thro' ilka bore the beams were glancing;
And loud resounded mirth and dancing.
  Inspiring bold John Barleycorn!
What dangers thou canst make us scorn!
Wi' tippenny, we fear nae evil;
Wi' usquebae, we'll face the devil!
The swats sae ream'd in Tammie's noddle,
Fair play, he car'd na deils a boddle!

Thou art the life o' public haunts

But Maggie stood right sair astonish'd,
Till, by the heel and hand admonish'd,
She ventur'd forward on the light;
And, vow! Tam saw an unco sight!
Warlocks and witches in a dance!
Nae cotillon brent new frae France,
But hornpipes, jigs, strathspeys, and reels,
Put life and mettle in their heels.
A winnock-bunker in the east,
There sat auld Nick, in shape o' beast –
A touzie tyke, black, grim, and large!
To gie them music was his charge:
He screw'd the pipes and gart them skirl,
Till roof and rafters a' did dirl.
Coffins stood round like open presses,
That shaw'd the dead in their last dresses;
And by some devilish cantraip sleight
Each in its cauld hand held a light,
By which heroic Tam was able

To note upon the haly table
A murderer's banes in gibbet-airns;
Twa span-lang, wee, unchristen'd bairns;
A thief new-cutted frae the rape –
Wi' his last gasp his gab did gape;
Five tomahawks, wi' blude red rusted;
Five scymitars, wi' murder crusted;
A garter, which a babe had strangled;
A knife, a father's throat had mangled,
Whom his ain son o' life bereft –
The gray hairs yet stack to the heft;
Wi' mair of horrible and awfu',
Which even to name wad be unlawfu'.
  As Tammie glowr'd, amaz'd, and curious,
The mirth and fun grew fast and furious:
The piper loud and louder blew;
The dancers quick and quicker flew;
They reel'd, they set, they cross'd, they cleekit,
Till ilka carlin swat and reekit,

Their sarks, instead o' creeshie flannen.
Been snaw-white seventeen hunder linen!
Thir breeks o' mine, my only pair,
That ance were plush, o' gude blue hair,
I wad hae gi'en them off my hurdies,
For ae blink o' the bonnie burdies!

But wither'd beldams, auld and droll,
Rigwoodie hags wad spean a foal,
Louping and flinging on a crummock,
I wonder didna turn thy stomach.

But Tam kent what was what fu' brawlie
There was ae winsome wench and walie
That night enlisted in the core,
Lang after kent on Carrick shore!
(For mony a beast to dead she shot,
And perish'd mony a bonnie boat,
And shook baith meikle corn and bear,
And kept the country-side in fear.)
Her cutty sark, o' Paisley harn,

That while a lassie she had worn,
In longitude tho' sorely scanty,
It was her best, and she was vauntie.
Ah! little kent thy reverend grannie
That sark she coft for her wee Nannie
Wi' twa pund Scots ('twas a' her riches)
Wad ever grac'd a dance of witches!

But here my muse her wing maun cour;
Sic flights are far beyond her pow'r –
To sing how Nannie lap and flang,
(A souple jade she was, and strang);
And how Tam stood, like ane bewitch'd,
And thought his very een enrich'd;
Even Satan glowr'd, and fidg'd fu' fain,
And hotch'd and blew wi' might and main:
Till first ae caper, syne anither,
Tam tint his reason a' thegither,
And roars out 'Weel done, Cutty-sark!'
And in an instant all was dark!

Robert Burns and his creations

And scarcely had he Maggie rallied,
When out the hellish legion sallied.
  As bees bizz out wi' angry fyke
When plundering herds assail their byke,

As open pussie's mortal foes
When pop! she starts before their nose,
As eager runs the market-crowd,
When 'Catch the thief!' resounds aloud.
So Maggie runs; the witches follow,
Wi' mony an eldritch skriech and hollow.
  Ah, Tam! ah, Tam! thou'll get thy fairin'!
In hell they'll roast thee like a herrin'!
In vain thy Kate awaits thy comin'!
Kate soon will be a woefu' woman!
Now do thy speedy utmost, Meg,
And win the key-stane o' the brig:
There at them thou thy tail may toss,
A running stream they darena cross.
But ere the key-stane she could make,

The fient a tail she had to shake!
For Nannie, far before the rest,
Hard upon noble Maggie prest,
And flew at Tam wi' furious ettle;
But little wist she Maggie's mettle!
Ae spring brought off her master hale,
But left behind her ain gray tail:
The carlin claught her by the rump,
And left poor Maggie scarce a stump.

Now, wha this tale o' truth shall read,
Each man and mother's son, take heed;
Whene'er to drink you are inclin'd,
Or cutty-sarks rin in your mind,
Think! ye may buy the joys o'er dear;
Remember Tam o' Shanter's mare.

O thou unknown Almighty Cause
Of all my hope and fear!

❧ DEATH ☙

The Death and Dying Words of Poor Mailie, the Author's only Pet Yowe.

As Mailie, an' her lambs thegither,
Was ae day nibbling on the tether,
Upon her cloot she coost a hitch,
An' owre she warsled in the ditch;
There, groaning, dying, she did lie,
When Hughoc he cam doytin by.
  Wi' glowrin' een, an' lifted han's,
Poor Hughoc like a statue stan's;
He saw her days were near-hand ended,
But, wae's my heart! he could na mend it!
He gaped wide, but naething spak;
At length poor Mailie silence brak: –

'O thou, whase lamentable face
Appears to mourn my woefu' ease!
My dying words attentive hear,
An' bear them to my Master dear.
'Tell him, if e'er again he keep
As muckle gear as buy a sheep, –
O bid him never tie them mair
Wi' wicked strings o' hemp or hair!
But ca' them out to park or hill,
An' let them wander at their will;
So may his flock increase, an' grow
To scores o' lambs, an' packs o' woo!
'Tell him he was a Master kin',
An' aye was guid to me an' mine;
An' now my dying charge I gie him,
My helpless lambs, I trust them wi' him.
'O bid him save their harmless lives
Frae dogs, an' tods, an' butchers' knives!
But gie them guid cow-milk their fill,
Till they be fit to fend themsel:

An' tent them duly, e'en an' morn,
Wi' teats o' hay an' ripps o' corn.
'An' may they never learn the gates
Of ither vile wanrestfu' pets –
To slink thro' slaps, an' reave an' steal,
At stacks o' pease, or stocks o' kail.
So may they, like their great forbears,
For mony a year come thro' the shears;
So wives will gie them bits o' bread,
An' bairns greet for them when they're dead.
'My poor tup-lamb, my son an' heir,
O bid him breed him up wi' care!
An', if he live to be a beast,
To pit some havins in his breast!
An' warn him, what I winna name,
To stay content wi' yowes at hame;
An' no to rin an' wear his cloots,
Like ither menseless graceless brutes.

'An' neist my yowie, silly thing,
Gude keep thee frae a tether string!
O may thou ne'er forgather up
Wi' ony blastit moorland tup;
But ay keep mind to moop an' mell,
Wi' sheep o' credit like thysel!

'And now, my bairns, wi' my last breath
I lea'e my blessin wi' you baith;
An' when you think upo' your mither,
Mind to be kind to ane anither.

'Now, honest Hughoc, dinna fail
To tell my master a' my tale;
An' bid him burn this cursed tether;
An', for thy pains, thou'se get my blether.'

This said, poor Mailie turn'd her head,
An' closed her een amang the dead!

The house in Dumfries where Burns died

Macpherson's Farewell

Farewell, ye dungeons dark and strong,
The wretch's destinie:
Macpherson's time will not be long
On yonder gallows tree.

Sae rantingly, sae wantonly,
Sae dauntingly gaed he;
He played a spring and danced it round,
Below the gallows tree.

Oh, what is death but parting breath?
On mony a bloody plain
I've dared his face, and in this place
I scorn him yet again!

Untie these bands from off my hands,
And bring to me my sword,
And there's no a man in all Scotland,
But I'll brave him at a word.

I've lived a life of sturt and strife;
I die by treacherie:
It burns my heart I must depart
And not avengèd be.

Now farewell light, thou sunshine bright,
And all beneath the sky!
May coward shame distain his name,
The wretch that dares not die!

A Prayer in the Prospect of Death

O Thou unknown Almighty Cause
  Of all my hope and fear!
In whose dread presence, ere an hour,
  Perhaps I must appear!

If I have wander'd in those paths
  Of life I ought to shun;
As something, loudly in my breast,
  Remonstrates I have done;

Thou know'st that Thou hast formèd me
  With passions wild and strong;
And list'ning to their witching voice
  Has often led me wrong.

Where human weakness has come short,
  Or frailty stept aside,
Do thou, All-Good! for such Thou art,
  In shades of darkness hide.

Where with intention I have err'd,
  No other plea I have,
But Thou art good; and Goodness still
  Delighteth to forgive.

'Clarinda', one of Burns' sweethearts

❧ LOVE ☙

The Birks of Aberfeldy

Bonnie lassie, will ye go,
Will yo go, will ye go,
Bonnie lassie, will ye go
  To the Birks of Aberfeldy?

Now simmer blinks on flowery braes,
And o'er the crystal streamlet plays,
Come let us spend the lightsome days
  In the Birks of Aberfeldy.

While o'er their heads the hazels hing,
The little birdies blythely sing,
Or lightly flit on wanton wing
  In the Birks of Aberfeldy.

The braes ascend like lofty wa's,
The foaming stream deep-roaring fa's,
O'erhung wi' fragrant spreading shaws –
  The Birks of Aberfeldy.

The hoary cliffs are crown'd wi' flowers,
White o'er the linns the burnie pours,
And rising, weets wi' misty showers
  The Birks of Aberfeldy.

Let fortune's gifts at random flee,
They ne'er shall draw a wish frae me,
Supremely blest wi' love and thee,
  In the Birks of Aberfeldy.

Now simmer blinks on flowery braes
And o'er the crystal streamlet plays

Lord Gregory

O mirk, mirk is this midnight hour,
  And loud the tempest's roar;
A waefu' wanderer seeks thy tow'r,
  Lord Gregory, ope thy door.

An exile frae her father's ha',
  And a' for loving thee;
At least some pity on me shaw,
  If love it mayna be.

Lord Gregory, mind'st thou not the grove,
  By bonnie Irwine side,
Where first I own'd that virgin love
  I lang lang had denied?

How aften didst thou pledge and vow
  Thou wad for aye be mine!
And my fond heart, itsel sae true,
  It ne'er mistrusted thine.

Hard is thy heart, Lord Gregory,
  And flinty is thy breast:
Thou bolt of heaven that flashest by,
  O wilt thou give me rest!

Ye mustering thunders from above,
  Your willing victim see!
But spare, and pardon my fause love,
  His wrangs to heaven and me!

Burns and Highland Mary

The Rigs O' Barley

It was upon a Lammas night,
   When corn rigs are bonnie,
Beneath the moon's unclouded light
   I held awa to Annie:
The time flew by wi' tentless heed,
   Till 'tween the late and early,
Wi' sma' persuasion she agreed
   To see me thro' the barley.

The sky was blue, the wind was still,
   The moon was shining clearly;
I set her down wi' right good will
   Amang the rigs o' barley;
I kent her heart was a' my ain;
   I loved her most sincerely;
I kissed her owre and owre again
   Amang the rigs o' barley

I locked her in my fond embrace;
Her heart was beating rarely;
My blessings on that happy place,
Amang the rigs o' barley!
But by the moon and stars so bright,
That shone that hour so clearly,
She aye shall bless that happy night
Amang the rigs o' barley.

I hae been blythe wi' comrades dear;
I hae been merry drinking;
I hae been joyfu' gatherin' gear;
I hae been happy thinking:
But a' the pleasures e'er I saw,
Tho' three times doubled fairly,
That happy night was worth them a;
Amang the rigs o' barley.

Corn rigs, an' barley rigs,
An' corn rigs are bonnie:
I'll ne'er forget that happy night,
Amang the rigs wi' Annie.

Green Grow the Rashes

Green grow the rashes O,
   Green grow the rashes O;
The sweetest hours that e'er I spend,
   Are spent amang the lasses O!

There's nought but care on ev'ry han',
   In ev'ry hour that passes O;
What signifies the life o' man,
   An' 'twere na for the lasses O.

The warly race may riches chase,
   An' riches still may fly them O;
An' tho' at last they catch them fast,
   Their hearts can ne'er enjoy them O.

But gie me a canny hour at e'en,
My arms about my dearie O;
An' warly cares, an' warly men,
May a' gao tapsalteerie O!

For you sae douce, ye sneer at this,
Ye're nought but senseless asses O:
The wisest man the warl' saw,
He dearly lov'd the lasses O.

Auld nature swears, the lovely dears
Her noblest work she classes O;
Her prentice han' she tried on man,
An' then she made the lasses O.

Illustration to 'Auld Lang Syne'

O, Were I on Parnassus' Hill!

O, were I on Parnassus' hill,
Or had of Helicon my fill!
That I might catch poetic skill,
  To sing how dear I love thee.
But Nith maun be my Muse's well,
My Muse maun be thy bonnie sel;
On Corsincon I'll glowr and spell,
  And write how dear I love thee.

Then come, sweet Muse, inspire my lay!
For a' the lee-lang simmer's day,
I could na sing, I could na say,
  How much, how dear, I love thee.
I see thee dancing o'er the green,
Thy waist sae jimp, thy limbs sae clean,
Thy tempting looks, thy roguish een –
  By Heaven and earth I love thee!

By night, by day, a-field, at hame,
The thoughts o' thee my breast inflame
And aye I muse and sing thy name –
  I only live to love thee.
Tho' I were doom'd to wander on,
Beyond the sea, beyond the sun,
Till my last weary sand was run;
  Till then – and then I'd love thee.

Burns' quaich, knife and fork

Coming Through the Rye

Coming through the rye, poor body,
  Coming through the rye,
She draiglet a' her petticoatie,
  Coming through the rye.

Gin a body meet a body
  Coming through the rye;
Gin a body kiss a body,
  Need a body cry?

Gin a body meet a body
  Coming through the glen;
Gin a body kiss a body,
  Need the world ken?

Jenny's a' wat, poor body;
  Jenny's seldom dry;
She draiglet a' her petticoatie,
  Coming through the rye.

Go Fetch to me a Pint O' Wine

Go fetch to me a pint o' wine,
  An' fill it in a silver tassie;
That I may drink, before I go,
  A service to my bonnie lassie.
The boat rocks at the pier o' Leith.
  Fu' loud the wind blaws frae the ferry,
The ship rides by the Berwick-law,
  And I mann leave my bonnie Mary.

The trumpets sound, the banners fly,
  The glittering spears are rankèd ready;
The shouts o' war are heard afar,
  The battle closes thick and bloody;
But it's no the roar o' sea or shore
  Wad mak me langer wish to tarry;
Nor shout o' war that's heard afar,
  It's leaving thee, my bonnie Mary.

My Love is Like a Red Red Rose

My love is like a red red rose
  That's newly sprung in June:
My love is like the melodie
  That's sweetly play'd in tune.

So fair art thou, my bonnie lass,
  So deep in love am I:
And I will love thee still, my dear,
  Till a' the seas gang dry.

Till a' the seas gang dry, my dear.
  And the rocks melt wi' the sun:
And I will love thee still, my dear,
  While the sands o' life shall run.

And fare thee weel, my only love,
  And fare thee weel awhile!
And I will come again, my love,
  Tho' it were ten thousand mile.

❧ FRIENDSHIP ☙

Epistle to Hugh Parker

In this strange land, this uncouth clime,
A land unknown to prose or rhyme;
Where words ne'er crost the Muse's heckles,
Nor limpit in poetic shackles;
A land that prose did never view it,
Except when drunk he stacher't through it;
Here, ambush'd by the chimla cheek,
Hid in an atmosphere of reek,
I hear a wheel thrum i' the neuk,
I hear it – for in vain I leuk.
The red poat gleams, a fiery kernel,
Enhusked by a fog infernal;
Here, for my wonted rhyming raptures,

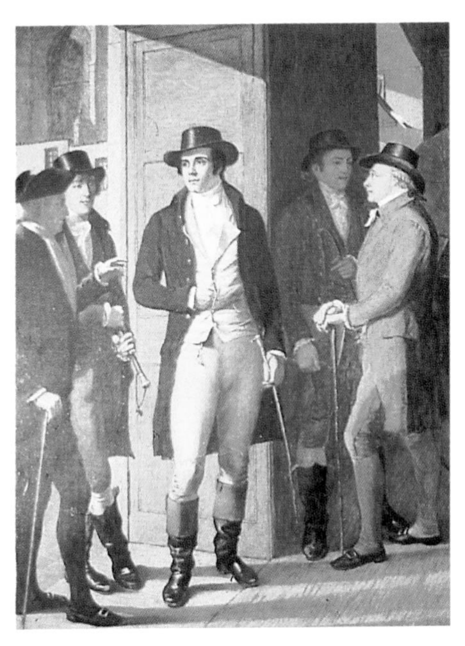

Burns and Scott in Sibbald's Library, W B Johnstone

I sit and count my sins by chapters;
For life and spunk like ither Christians,
I'm dwindled down to mere existence,
Wi' nae converse but Gallowa' bodies,
Wi' nae kend face but Jenny Geddes.
Jenny, my Pegasean pride!
Dowie she saunters down Nithside,
And ay a westlin leuk she throws,
While tears hap o'er her auld brown nose!
Was it for this, wi' canny care,
Thou bure the Bard through many a shire?
At howes or hillocks never stumbled,
And late or early never grumbled?

O, had I power like inclination,
I'd heeze thee up a constellation,
To canter with the Sagitarre,
Or loup the ecliptic like a bar;
Or turn the pole like any arrow;
Or, when auld Phoebus bids good-morrow,
Down the zodiac urge the race,
And cast dirt on his godship's face;
For I could lay my bread and kail
He'd ne'er cast saut upo' thy tail.
Wi' a' this care and a' this grief,
And sma', sma' prospect of relief,
And nought but peat reek i' my head,
How can I write what ye can read?
Tarbolton, twenty-fourth o' June,
Ye'll find me in a better tune;
But till we meet and weet our whistle,
Tak this excuse for nae epistle.

View of Edinburgh in Burns' time

Epistle to a Young Friend

I lang hae thought, my youthfu' friend,
  A something to have sent you,
Tho' it should serve nae ither end
  Than just a kind memento;
But how the subject theme may gang,
  Let time and chance determine;
Perhaps it may turn out a sang,
  Perhaps turn out a sermon.

Ye'll try the world soon, my lad,
  And, Andrew dear, believe me,
Ye'll find mankind an unco squad,
  And muckle they may grieve ye:

For care and trouble set your thought,
  Ev'n when your end's attained;
And a' your views may come to nought,
  Where ev'ry nerve is strained.

I'll no say men are villains a';
  The real harden'd wicked,
Wha hae nae check but human law,
  Are to a few restricked:
But oh! mankind are unco weak,
  An' little to be trusted;
If self the wavering balance shake,
  It's rarely right adjusted!

Yet they wha fa' in fortune's strife,
  Their fate we shouldna censure;
For still th' important end of life
  They equally may answer.
A man may hae an honest heart,
  Tho' poortith hourly stare him;
A man may tak a neibor's part.
  Yet hae nae cash to spare him.

Aye free, aff han', your story tell,
   When wi' a bosom crony;
But still keep something to yoursel
   Ye scarcely tell to ony.
Conceal yoursel as weel's ye can
   Frae critical dissection;
But keek thro' ev'ry other man
   Wi' sharpen'd sly inspection.

The sacred lowe o' weel-plac'd love,
   Luxuriantly indulge it;
But never tempt th' illicit rove,
   Tho' naething should divulge it:
I wave the quantum o' the sin,
   The hazard of concealing;
But oh! it hardens a' within,
   And petrifies the feeling!

To catch dame Fortune's golden smile,
  Assiduous wait upon her;
And gather gear by ev'ry wile
  That's justified by honour;
Not for to hide it a hedge,
  Nor for a train attendant;
But for the glorious privilege
  Of being independent.

The fear o' hell's a hangman's whip
  To haud the wretch in order;
But where ye feel your honour grip,
  Let that aye be your border:
Its slightest touches, instant pause –
  Debar a' side pretences;
And resolutely keep its laws,
  Uncaring consequences.

Illustration to 'The Cotter's Saturday Night'

The great Creator to revere
Must sure become the creature;
But still the preaching cant forbear,
And ev'n the rigid feature:
Yet ne'er with wits profane to range
Be complaisance extended;
An atheist laugh's a poor exchange
For Deity offended.

When ranting round in pleasure's ring,
Religion may be blinded;
Or, if she gie a random sting,
It may be little minded;
But when on life we're tempest-driv'n,
A conscience but a canker –
A correspondence fix'd wi' Heav'n
Is sure a noble anchor.

Adieu, dear amiable youth!
  Your heart can ne'er be wanting!
May prudence, fortitude, and truth
  Erect your brow undaunting.
In ploughman phrase, God send you speed
  Still daily to grow wiser;
And may ye better reck the rede
  Than ever did th' adviser!

Two drovers stop for the night

Ah, Chloris

Ah, Chloris, since it may na be,
  That thou of love wilt hear;
If from the lover thou maun flee,
  Yet let the friend be dear.

Altho' I love my Chloris mair
  Than ever tongue could tell;
My passion I will ne'er declare,
  I'll say I wish thee well:

Tho' a' my daily care thou art,
  And a' my nightly dream,
I'll hide the struggle in my heart,
  And say it is esteem.

Auld Lang Syne

Should auld acquaintance be forgot,
And never brought to min'?
Should auld acquaintance be forgot,
And auld lang syne?

For auld lang syne, my dear.
For auld lang syne,
We'll tak a cup o' kindness yet,
For auld lang syne.

We twa hae run about the braes,
And pu'd the gowans fine;
But we've wander'd mony a weary foot
Sin' auld lang syne.

We twa hae paidled i' the burn,
From morning sun till dine;
But seas between us braid hae roar'd
Sin' auld lang syne.

And there's a hand, my trusty fiere,
And gie's a hand o' thine;
And we'll tak a right guid-willie waught,
For auld lang syne.

And surely ye'll be your pint-stowp,
And surely I'll be mine;
And we'll tak a cup o' kindness yet
For auld lang syne.

❧ MARRIAGE ❧

Tam Glen

My heart is a breaking, dear Tittie,
  Some counsel unto me come len',
To anger them a' is a pity;
  But what will I do wi' Tam Glen?

I'm thinking, wi' sic a braw fellow,
  In poortith I might mak a fen';
What care I in riches to wallow,
  If I maunna marry Tam Glen?

There's Lowrie the laird o' Dumeller,
  'Guid-day to you, brute!' he comes ben:
He brags and he blaws o' his siller,
  But when will he dance like Tam Glen?

The Wounded Hound, Sir Edwin Landseer

My minnie does constantly deave me,
  And bids me beware o' young men;
They flatter, she says, to deceive me;
  But wha can think sae o' Tam Glen?

My daddie says, gin I'll forsake him,
  He'll gie me guid hunder marks ten:
But, if it's ordain'd I maun take him,
  O wha will I get but Tam Glen?

Yestreen at the Valentines' dealing,
  My heart to my mou gied a sten:
For thrice I drew ane without failing,
  And thrice it was written, Tam Glen.

The last Halloween I was waukin'
  My droukit sark-sleeve, as ye ken;
His likeness cam up the house stalkin' –
  And the very grey breeks o' Tam Glen!

Come, counsel, dear Tittie, don't tarry;
  I'll gie you my bonnie black hen,
Gif ye will advise me to marry
  The lad I lo'e dearly, Tam Glen.

John Anderson My Jo

John Anderson my jo, John,
  When we were first acquent,
Your locks were like the raven,
  Your bonnie brow was brent;
But now your brow is beld, John,
  Your locks are like the snow;
But blessings on your frosty pow,
  John Anderson, my jo.

John Anderson my jo, John,
  We clamb the hill thegither;
And mony a canty day, John,
  We've had wi' ane anither:
Now we maun totter down, John,
  And hand in hand we'll go,
And sleep thegither at the foot,
  John Anderson, my jo.

Willie's Wife

Willie Wastle dwalt on Tweed,
  The spot they ca'd it Linkumdoddie;
Willie was a wabster guid,
  Cou'd stown a cluo wi' ony body.
He had a wife was dour and din,
  O Tinkler Madgie was her mither;
Sie a wife as Willie had,
  I wad na gie a button for her!

She has an ee, she has but ane,
  The cat has twa the very colour:
Five rusty teeth, forbye a stump,
  A clapper tongue wad deave a miller;
A whiskin beard about her mou,
  Her nose and chin they threaten ither;
Sie a wife, &c.

She's bow-hough'd, she's hein shinn'd,
Ae limpin leg a hand-breed shorter;
She's twisted right, she's twisted left,
To balance fair in ilka quarter:
She has a hump upon her breast,
The twin o' that upon her shouther;
Sic a wife, &c.

Auld baudrons by the ingle sits,
An' wi' her loof her face a-washin;
But Willie's wife is nae sae trig,
She dights her grunzie wi' a hushion;
Her walie nieves like midden-creels,
Her face wad fyle the Logan-water;
Sic a wife as Willie had,
I wad na gie a button for her!

Duncan Gray

Duncan Gray came here to woo,
Ha, ha, the wooing o't,
On blythe Yule night when we were fou,
Ha, ha, the wooing o't.
Maggie coost her head fu' heigh,
Look'd asklent and unco skeigh,
Gart poor Duncan stand abeigh;
Ha, ha, the wooing o't.

Duncan fleech'd, and Duncan pray'd;
Ha, ha, the wooing o't,
Meg was deaf as Ailsa Craig,
Ha, ha, the wooing o't.
Duncan sigh'd baith out and in,
Grat his een baith bleer't and blin',
Spak o' lowpin o'er a linn;
Ha, ha, the wooing o't.

Time and chance are but a tide,
    Ha, ha, the wooing o't,
Slighted love is sair to bide,
    Ha, ha, the wooing o't.
Shall I, like a fool, quoth he,
For a haughty hizzie die?
She may gae to – France for me!
    Ha, ha, the wooing o't.

How it comes let doctors tell,
    Ha, ha, the wooing o't,
Meg grew sick as he grew haill,
    Ha, ha, the wooing o't.
Something in her bosom wrings,
For relief a sigh she brings;
And O, her een they spak sic things!
    Ha, ha, the wooing o't.

Duncan was a lad o' grace,
        Ha, ha, the wooing o't,
Maggio's was a piteous case,
        Ha, ha, the wooing o't.
Duncan couldna be her death,
Swelling pity smoor'd his wrath;
Now they're crouse and cantie baith!
        Ha, ha, the wooing o't.

Epitaph on a Henpecked Country Squire

As father Adam first was fooled
    (A case that's still too common),
Here lies a man a woman ruled,
    – The Devil ruled the woman.

❧ ANIMALS ☙

To a Mouse, on Turning Her up in Her Nest with the Plough, November, 1785.

Wee, sleekit, cow'rin', tim'rous beastie,
O what a panic's in thy breastie!
Thon need na start awa sae hasty,
        Wi' bickering brattle!
I wad be laith to rin an' chase thee
        Wi' murd'ring pattle!

I'm truly sorry man's dominion
Has broken Nature's social union,
An' justifis that ill opinion
        Which makes thee startle
At me, thy poor earth-born companion,
        An' fellow-mortal!

I doubt na, whiles, but thon may thieve;
What then? poor beastie, thou maun live!
A daimen-icker in a thrave
        'S a sma' request:
I'll get a blessin' wi' the lave,
        And never miss't!

Thy wee bit housie, too, in ruin!
Its silly wa's the win's are strewin'!
An' maething, now, to big a new ane,
        O' foggage green!
        An' bleak December's winds ensuin',
Baith snell an' keen!

Thou saw the fields laid bare and waste,
An' weary winter comin' fast,
An' cozie here, beneath the blast,
        Thou thought to dwell,
Till crash! the cruel coulter past
        Out-thro' thy cell.

That wee bit heap o' leaves an' stibble
Has cost thee mony a weary nibble!
Now thou's turn'd out, for a' thy trouble,
        But house or hald,
To thole the winter's sleety dribble,
        Am' cranreuch cauld!

But, Mousie, thou art no thy lane,
In proving foresight may be vain:
The best laid schemes o' mice an' men
        Gang aft a-gley,
An' lea'e us nought but grief an' pain
        For promis'd joy.

Still thou art blest compar'd wi' me!
The present only toucheth thee:
But oh! I backward cast my e'e
        On prospects drear!
An' forward tho' I canna see,
        I guess an' fear!